015

SPIRIT OF
THE EAST LANCASHIRE RAILWAY

MIKE & KARL HEATH

First published in Great Britain in 2010

British Library Cataloguing-in-Publication Data
A CIP record for this title is available from the British Library

ISBN 978 1 906887 66 7

PiXZ Books
Halsgrove House, Ryelands Industrial Estate,
Bagley Road, Wellington, Somerset TA21 9PZ
Tel: 01823 653777
Fax: 01823 216796
email: sales@halsgrove.com

An imprint of Halstar Ltd, part of the Halsgrove group of companies
Information on all Halsgrove titles is available at: www.halsgrove.com

Printed and bound in China by Toppan Leefung Printing Ltd

Introduction

The Manchester, Bury and Rossendale Railway was established in 1844 to serve the cotton mills in the Irwell Valley. Two years later it became the East Lancashire Railway and that title lasted until 1859 when the company was absorbed into the Lancashire and Yorkshire Railway.

Today the name lives on as the preservation society that has restored the section from Bury to Rawtenstall, in the heart of Rossendale at the northern end of the Irwell Valley, and to Heywood in an easterly direction. The line passes over high viaducts, through long tunnels and along a wonderfully varied countryside where a legacy of industrial architecture is set amongst a landscape of busy market towns, quiet riverside woodland and grazing meadows, with rugged moorland fells above.

In a relatively short preservation lifetime, assisted by the local authorities, the society has re-opened these lines, restored or totally rebuilt the infrastructure and created an attractive 12-mile long preserved railway that has attracted a great variety of steam locomotives, from all over the country, to haul their trains.

What follows is a photographic journey recording the line at work throughout all seasons, day and night, the wonderfully varied landscape through which it passes and many of the locomotives that have visited in recent years. A combination that has made the railway one of the most popular in the country.

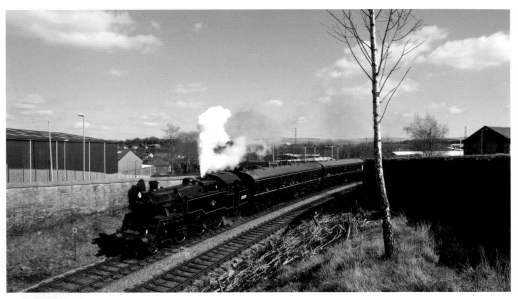

Reached in September 2003 Heywood is the current eastern terminus of the line. The journey begins with British Railway Standard 4 tank 2-6-4 No. 80098, a popular visitor from the Midland Railway Centre, easing a train out on a bright March morning in 2009.

Ex-LMS 'Jinty' No. 47324 a mainstay of services, since emerging from restoration, attacks the 1 in 80 gradient of Broadfield Bank out of Bury with a service for Heywood.

Left:
Well away from its native Scottish Highlands ex-LNER K4 class No. 61994 'The Great Marquess' makes easy work of this autumn 2008 train as it scurries to Heywood.

Right:
No. 92214, a member of the celebrated British Railways 9F class, coasts over Roche Viaduct.

Roche Viaduct is an impressive 7-arch structure which carries the railway over the River Roche. 'The Great Marquess' forges its way towards Heywood with the first train of the day on a crisp 1 November 2008.

Since re-opening, the East Lancashire Railway has played host to many prestigious visitors. In March 2007 National Railway Museum owned ex-Southern Railway 4-6-0 No. 850 'Lord Nelson' visited after overhaul.

Descending the 'ski slope', having successfully crossed the humpback bridge over the Manchester Metrolink System, Wemyss Private Railway No. 15 'Earl David' approaches Bury Bolton Street station.

Unique B.R. Standard Class 8P No. 71000 'Duke of Gloucester' departing Bury for Heywood with a train that includes the chocolate and cream liveried dining coaches.

The railway's shed is at Buckley Wells and at the end of the day's work No. 71000 rests with Standard 4 No. 76079 and 'Black Five' No. 45407 'The Lancashire Fusilier'.

Left:
Since 1993 the railway's locomotive department has been based in the former ex-British Rail Electric Car shop at Buckley Wells. The shed itself forms the backdrop in this scene as No. 76079 and 'Duke of Gloucester' cool down after a day's work.

Right:
In the early days of preservation the railway relied on ex-industrial tank engines to haul most services. The presence of such engines on the line continues today. At the April 2009 gala diminutive 0-4-0 ST 'May' storms through Bury station with a demonstration freight.

Left:
The railway's ex-LMS 'Jinty' No. 47324 waits in Bury station's platform No.2, basking in the sunshine after the rain with a freight train.

Right:
Gala weekends see services operating into the evening. At dusk on 24 January 2009 the driver of 'Black Five' No. 45407 awaits the signal from the guard before departing.

The crew of 76079 look on as the station master gives the guard of this Heywood-bound train permission to 'green flag' departure to Heywood.

A Rawtenstall service departs from platform 4 in the hands of Standard Class 4 tank No. 80098 in the guise of scrapped classmate No. 80086.

Early morning freights are a feature of gala weekends. In April 2009 the standard tank charges through Burrs Country Park at 8am.

Ex-Lancashire & Yorkshire Railway 0-6-0 tender engine No. 1300 wears the elegant livery of that company, offering a pleasing alternative to British Railways' colours. Lit by a shaft of sunlight on a stormy afternoon it passes Burrs with a shuttle service to Ramsbottom.

Standard tank No. 80098 was a regular performer during the first half of 2009 and its duties would usually include the Sunday 1.10pm departure from Bury. This train often has the 'Lancastrian' dining train added at the rear. On this occasion a day of fine sunshine welcomed diners to the Irwell Valley.

Looking the other way we see south-facing double-headed 'Black Fives' No. 45231 'Sherwood Forester' and No. 45407 'The Lancashire Fusilier' powering a train through Burrs with a Bury-bound train.

With frost on the ground and the steam hanging in the cold January 2009 air, 80098 is seen on a dawn freight.

A month later, and a few degrees warmer, No. 1300 bustles its freight train north.

With the railway predominantly running North-South, Burrs is an excellent location to capture a silhouette of a train. 25 January 2009 provided a clear sky as a backdrop to this view of Black Five 45231 on a Rawtenstall service.

Former Wemyss Private Railway No. 15 'Earl David' was hired in to ease a locomotive shortage in the middle part of 2009 and it made a fine sight racing through Burrs on the afternoon of 13 September.

Black 5 No. 45407 'The Lancashire Fusilier' has a long association with the railway and the popular engine is seen here steaming towards Summerseat station on a morning train.

The driver of 80086 (aka 80098) watches the road ahead as they hurry a freight down the valley. Summerseat station can just be seen in the distance.

Another engine with a long history at the East Lancs is Standard 4 2-6-0 No. 76079, captured here sprinting through the sweeping bends near Summerseat. However, this locomotive has now moved across the Pennines to the North Yorkshire Moors Railway and is featured in the Halsgrove publications on that line.

Left:
Spring in the Irwell Valley and the Daffodils are in bloom as two walkers acknowledge the crossing's warning signs and watch 80098 pass by.

Right:
No. 61994 'The Great Marquess' makes a spirited departure from Summerseat with a Heywood-bound service as the surrounding trees show the first colours of autumn 2008.

Another National Railway Museum-owned locomotive to visit East Lancashire is the former Great Western Railway's 'City of Truro', reputed to be the first locomotive to reach 100 miles per hour, a feat achieved in 1904.

Summer 2008 is in full cry with lush green foliage to greet this train handled by one of the railway's heritage diesels. On this occasion it's Class 40 No. D335.

Left:
Returning to spring and the crossing seen on page 32 to view No. 47324 and a matching rake of maroon coaches heading for Bury.

Right:
An appropriate visitor to the 2009 1940s weekend was this United States Army Transport Corp (USATC) S160 No. 5197, which is usually based on the Churnet Valley Railway. The flags adorning the smokebox denote the presence of VIPs on the train including Franklin D. Roosevelt and Winston Churchill who were on their way to inspect troops at Irwell Vale.

Left:
In autumn 2007 the trees in the valley turned all shades of red and orange which provided a stark contrast to the apple green livery of LNER V2 No. 4771 'Green Arrow'. The engine was at the railway in November 2007 as part of its farewell tour before being withdrawn from service and returning to the National Railway Museum in York.

Right:
March 2007 and 'Lord Nelson' coasts south over Brooksbottom Viaduct preparing to stop at Summerseat station.

Early morning is the best time to photograph the east side of the viaduct. Another of the line's diesels, Class 47 No. 47402 'Gateshead' rumbles over the River Irwell. This locomotive and section of line were used in the BBC's series 'Life on Mars' for the final episode of series two.

An azure blue sky greeted 'Earl David' and its Rawtenstall-bound train
on the morning of 20 September 2009.

'The Red Rose' evening dining train offers a leisurely journey along the line and includes a pause on Brooksbottom Viaduct whilst diners enjoy their meal as the sun sets. On 29 May 2009 the duty of hauling the train fell to USATC S160 No. 5197 which glinted in the last rays of sunlight.

Left:
Leaving the viaduct behind 45407 continues up the valley towards Ramsbottom.

Right:
High summer 2009 and Class 33 D6526 'Captain Bill Smith RNR' is about to enter the 423-yard long Brooksbottom Tunnel, the parapet of which can be seen bottom left.

Left:
Class 40 D335 rests under the new canopy at Ramsbottom station.

Right:
Immediately north of the platforms at Ramsbottom is a level crossing here being negotiated by the 'Jinty' with a return working from Rawtenstall.

B.R. Standard Class 8P No. 71000 'Duke of Gloucester' prepares to leave.

Ramsbottom station with its recently completed canopy which was salvaged from a number of North-West stations. This scene is testament to the achievements of the railway and its volunteers who have created what you see here from the single barren platform left by BR when the railway closed.

Left:
Sunday 21 February 2001 dawned with a carpet of snow covering the valley. 45407 departs Ramsbottom and heads north on its way to the halt at Irwell Vale.

Right:
Another photograph from that wintry day depicting 'Crab' No. 42765 arriving at Irwell Vale. The viaduct in the left background used to carry the Haslingden line which had a junction with the ELR at Stubbins between Ramsbottom and Irwell Vale.

'The Great Marquess' slows to stop at Irwell Vale with an afternoon train from Rawtenstall.

Ex L&Y No. 1300 and 'Jinty' No. 47324 combine efforts to lift an eight coach Heywood-bound train away from Irwell Vale.

Left:
On arrival at Irwell Vale an armed guard protects the train we saw earlier conveying Churchill and Roosevelt during the 1940s weekend. The railway now holds two of these weekends a year to remember those who fought in the war and the role played by the railways during the conflict.

Right:
A long way from its spiritual home on western region branchlines ex-GWR 0-4-2 tank No. 1450 restarts from a frosty Irwell Vale in December 1998.

Left:
The platform and shelter at this location are preservation era constructions. In British Rail's day there was only a mill siding alongside the village.

Leaving the village of Irwell Vale behind USATC S160 5197 continues up the valley, but fails to impress the local livestock. They must have witnessed scenes like this many times!

Left:
At Ewood Bridge the trains work hard against the gradient and the field next to the road bridge is an ideal vantage point.

Right:
Another winter and more snow in the valley as Great Western Railway Hall class No. 4936 'Kinlet Hall', a visitor from Tyseley, makes its way to Rawtenstall.

LNER K4 No. 61994 'The Great Marquess' drifts down the valley heading back to Bury.
In the autumnal background is the village of Helmshore and the A56 trunk road.

A riverside walk from Ewood Bridge leads to this attractive location. The passing Black Five No. 45231 'The Sherwood Forester' and its newly painted maroon coaches are reflected in the meandering waters.

On the outskirts of Rawtenstall the railway passes between mills and again crosses over the river. 'Jinty' No. 47324 heads a Bury service away from the terminus.

As at Ramsbottom a derelict platform has received a new station building in an original railway style. A clock tower similar to the one that stood at Bury's Bolton Street station completes the structure.

The return journey commences with Black Five 45407 leaving Rawtenstall on a beautiful 19 April 2009, ahead lies 16 miles of an ever-changing landscape.